CW01336671

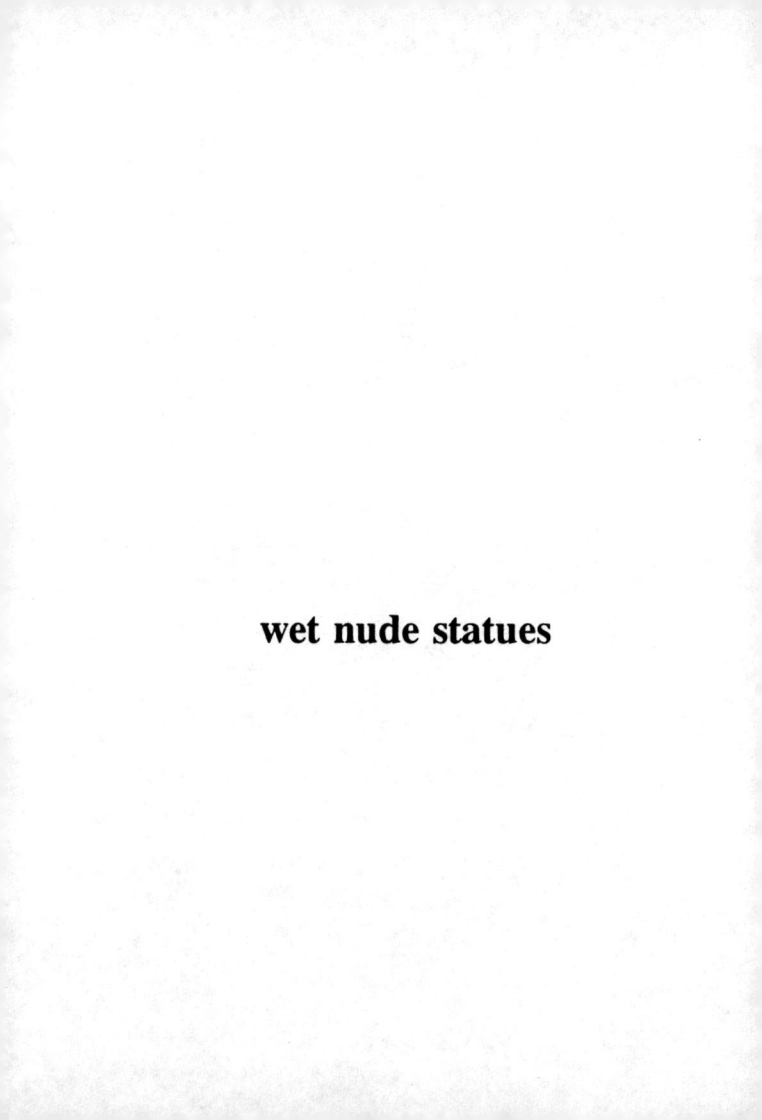

wet nude statues

wet nude statues

Colin Blundell

Cover: The back of the postcard on which the cover is based is so mutilated that the name and address of the French publisher to whom acknowledgement (and no doubt money) is due cannot be identified...

© Colin Blundell 1994

ISBN 1 870653 31 9

Hub Editions
11 The Ridgway
Flitwick
Bedfordshire
England MK45 1DH

January — October 1993

the gleaming pavement
swept—all the wet nude statues
go home to his lunch

(Postcard from Paris)

dark winter morning:
the people on the platform—
artificial light

coming out upon
a bay bathed in silver light—
you know the place well?

stoned out of their minds
on personal stereos
and newspaper words

sky with rising sun
passes by the train windows
riding up to town

call a spade a spade?
you can—I'd rather call it
a pomegranate

calling spades 'spades' is
not what a poet's about—
spades are pheasants' eggs

the evening love-in
cancelled—the teacher's got to
mark exercise books

down the station steps
every morning somebody
barges shouting "Shit!"

Jehovah's Witness
looking so miserable
& witnessing what?

yet another year
& the one dawn thrush singing:
its accustomed branch

early morning fog
& the train just departing;
a space created

the jangle of chains
and the gate opening wide—
thick fog on both sides

up on the Common
misty trees will be dripping
on the paths I knew well

our cat supposes
that she will live forever:
now comes endless night

cat's last day on earth
followed by millions of years
she'll spend under it

waiting forlorn for
the vet to come so the cat
can go into Night

& Monty the horse
comes to the cat's burial
by the silver birch

the great black Night Cat
is leaping across the sky
and the stars light up

old Albert says Spring's
coming: birds twittering in
the early morning

a flight of white gulls
against the newly-ploughed field
and the day goes on

curtains not drawn back
on an early winter's day
are at daggers drawn

a condom packet—
the early morning haiku
written on its flap

opacity curbs
but it also licenses
immense histories

those who swept the lawns
in Autumn now concentrate
on sweeping up snow

do you run these dreams
of past times through your mind too?
like I do   I mean

there's floating music
in the early shopping mall—
everybody floats

jovial starlings
clicking & whistling on roofs—
I whistle to them

the ambulance scream
makes all the platform people
suddenly silent

in the empty shed
all night the paint tins go pop
and the old roof creaks

the sun organised
on the lake to a straight line;
late evening in spring

lorry refugees:
children raise a hand to wave
on the mountain road

5.30 am:
Olivier Messiaen
in the Spring garden

the last lights of day:
the setting sun muzzed along
the lilac blossom

(after Harold Pinter: The Dwarfs)

red roofs organise
space & time by the sea-shore
and the wind is cold

on Sundays people
mow the lawn & wash the car
in preparation

tramp with plastic bags
stands in the road watching TV
in Barker's window

fly in the glue-pot
quickly abandons its ghost;
the planet spins on

old electric fire
discarded in the garden
heated by spring sun

the moon   this apple
identical as far as
the Earth is concerned

(after William James)

white gate   fence & barn
and then greenery stretching
to the horizon

in the old cabin
the wind is stirring curtains
and the day is poised

talk about wisdom—
endless possibilities;
birds in the forest

in ancient stillness
another weekend arrives
& then its over

the energetic
collecting broken branches—
the fire I'll enjoy

the meditation:
an old man's gift of glass ball;
the wasp still buzzing

familiar garden
(as down any alleyway)
its season constant

white hall & black beams
all becoming for a time
an angry wasp's buzz

dawn: a blackbird comes
to the patio puddle
& siphons water

the hot air balloon
drifts across my thinking field
and a cockerel sings

bumble-bee's wings click
in the straggly privet hedge—
sweet smell entrances

unexpected shower:
the sound of mowers ceases
till the cloud passes

thrush operating
in the snails' graveyard wiping
the carcass on stone

so many changes
to my essay on haiku—
now unreadable

from the privet top
to the silver birches' height
go racing white clouds

hedge & tree shadows
perambulate the bright lawn—
so does the reader

high wind in the trees
all day betokening rain
but nothing comes yet

& by the deck chair
a worn patch on the lush lawn—
riveting chapters

the noise of morning
pigeons hidden in the trees
& the eerie wind

especially clouds
galivanting all over—
then the homecoming

the evening's coming
in Russell Square—the typist
gone home to her meal

remote from traffic—
the shadow moving its pen;
the plane trees' mutter

folk sit in the Square
contemplating their next step—
the fountains turned off

people passing by
to their various venues—
such variety!

the negro pauses
transfixed by a shaft of sun
and closes his eyes

purple apples droop
above the newly-mown lawn;
the declining sun

the sky's single star—
my soul turns over its high
cold new morning thoughts

verticality
is all—what else makes the sun
rise up when it's dawn?

the newly-ploughed field
is fragmenting into sky
birds wheeling away

just the ticking clock
and evening sunlight patterns
moving on the wall

day in the garden—
getting it straight for Autumn
and our long absence

sunset projections
of net curtain flowers moving
between framed pictures

quantities of rooks
making a high dawn rumpus
in trees by the church

Autumn afternoon:
a mad poet's afternoon—
maple woods smoking

(after Hermann Melville: The Piazza)

early dawn   I sowed
the morning all before me—
golden rod signposts

(after Hermann Melville: The Piazza)

a winter wood road
all matted with winter-green
by pebbly waters

(after Hermann Melville: The Piazza)

red damsel-flies
basking on rocks by the pond—
the hot Autumn sun

one side of the pond
is occupied by Buddha—
I'm on the other

the modern harvest:
its roar invades garden peace
but not my quiet page

the rooks are cawing
home from their daily travels
to their own tree-tops

your ears can relax
when the combine harvester
pauses for turning

those bright pond moments
during all the Autumn day—
frog & damsel flies

sitting by the pond
the long Autumn afternoon—
& the sun moving round

late rooks fly over
trees by the church—warning cry
from incumbent rooks

the motorway jam
and the sunset comes & goes
while you're not looking

writing—metaphor
of the powder-fine substance
of the diverse world

(after Italo Calvino: Six Memos)

her perfume falling
from the bedroom she prepares
to do day's battle

all Sunday morning
the local pigeon shoot
battles with church bells

the summer-house lawn
is leaning into Autumn
broken willow-herb

millions of cobwebs
siphoning the morning mist—
the birds harping on

the river in flood
ten ducks washed up on the bank
shrugging off the shock

a quick glance behind:
the blue sky being shouldered
off by these storm clouds

reading sea haiku:
the sudden smell of full-tide
rising from the book

the whirring evening
turns into a flight of rooks
returning from fields

across my black scrawl
the scrawling of leaf shadows
by the Autumn sun

loud-speaker drumming
from outside the summer-house
but also the moon

dragon-fly passing
fossil-fly on this rock-face
and the time between?

(after Richard Jefferies)

from every grass-blade
& colour of butterflies—
the notes of my soul

(after Richard Jefferies)

working at a desk
in a dull office & then—
sunlight on the wall

cowl on a housetop
gathering as much outcome
as ceaseless labour

(after Richard Jefferies)

ten gulls enjoying
the river that's burst its banks;
elevated beaks

leaving the High Street
& hoping for a haiku
in the back turnings

the silent courtyard—
going out of it to find
the plane trees hissing

made of nothing—words;
just little performances
of tongue breath & lips

(John Fuller: The Worm and the Star)

beautiful girl's voice
singing down the long subway—
singing just for me!

blue sky in Autumn
promising another spring—
white clouds gathering

the wide silver road
out of Waterloo station—
o how many times?

people boarding trains
pierce the windows with their eyes—
then become normal

clouds floating along
past Battersea Power Station
no longer fuel fires

pains in my old bones
draw attention away from
the blue Autumn sky

up on the Common
the brown leaves are creating
another layer

long fascination:
other people's back gardens
& what they do there

with telescope eyes
searching the brightly lit rooms
seen from the railway

michaelmas daisies!
what a hole they bore into
my deep memory!

stag beetles flying
up The Avenue at dusk
forty years ago

gulls turning over
against a grey thundercloud
change from white to black

three magpies waiting
on the suburban platform
for jewels to alight

walking through the Park—
the old times and the old sun
are both in my mind

the sun slanting low
on massed Earlsfield chimney pots
and on yellow leaves

people leaving trains
turn their eyes to the exit
and pull their coats tight

look! the setting sun
making city offices
jubilant with light

& by North London
the sun is set behind cloud—
commuters yawning

burying their minds
in the Standard evening words
inventing the real

Hand Made
In
A Garden Shed
In
Bunyan Land